I Want A Leopard Gecko

Best Pets for Kids - Book 1

Tristan Pulsifer and
Jacquelyn Elnor Johnson

www.CrimsonHillBooks.com/best-pets-for-kids

First edition, September 2016.

Canadian Cataloguing in Publication Data

Pulsifer, Tristan and Johnson, Jacquelyn Elnor

I Want A Leopard Gecko

Best Pets For Kids Series

ISBN 978-0-9953191-2-7

1.Juvenile non-fiction. 2. Readers age 8 to 12. 3. Pet care. 4. Pet geckos. 5. Lizards. I. Title. II. Series.

Cover Photo: Jan Pietruszka via stockfresh.com

Book design: Jesse Johnson

Crimson Hill Books

(a division of)

Crimson Hill Products Inc.

Wolfville, Nova Scotia

Canada

Contents

<u>Introduction</u>

What is a Leopard Gecko?

This is a pet leopard gecko.

What is a gecko?

Geckos are one type of lizard.

All lizards are reptiles.

The reptile family includes turtles, alligators, crocodiles, snakes, birds and tuataras [here's how to

This is a wild tuatara.

say it: TOO-a-tare-ah]. Most wild reptiles live in many parts of the world, but tuataras are very rare. They live only in New Zealand.

Leopard geckos and tuataras look very different from each other. But they both have two things that every reptile has:

1. scales that cover at least part of their bodies,
2. they are cold-blooded (except for birds)

Cold-blooded means when they are too cold, they don't have any way to warm up their bodies.

When they're too hot, they don't sweat to cool off.

To get warm, cold-blooded creatures must find some heat, like going to sit in the sun.

When they are too hot, they have to find a cooler place.

If they can't do this, they will get very sick and might die.

Most of the world's creatures are cold-blooded. Only birds and mammals are warm-blooded.

Warm-blooded means they are able to make their own body heat. Horses, dogs, mice and people are all mammals.

Most reptiles do not make good pets. They want to live alone and be wild animals.

There are some reptiles that make great pets. One of the best for kids or new pet owners of any age is the leopard gecko.

Is a gecko like a snake?

Geckos and snakes are alike in some ways.

Both are reptiles.

Both live as wild animals or can be tamed as pets (though there are some types of lizards and also some types of snakes that make very bad pets!).

Both geckos and snakes have heads that are triangle-shaped.

Both shed their skins.

Both leopard geckos and some types of snakes have sharp teeth, but they can't chew their food. They have to swallow it whole.

This is a pet corn snake. Photo courtesy of Cynoclub via Stockfresh.

This little guy is a wild fire belly newt. Some newts look like small geckos, but all newts are amphibians.

Snakes can't close their eyes, but geckos can. Snakes don't have ears, but geckos do.

In times of danger, a gecko's tail falls off so it can escape. No snake can do this. A really amazing thing is that when a gecko's tail breaks off, it will quickly grow back.

Both snakes and geckos have a super sense of smell. Leopard geckos also have keen eyesight.

Is a gecko an amphibian?

No, amphibians are a different family group than reptiles.

The amphibian family includes frogs, toads and salamanders.

Some amphibians might look a little like reptiles, but this is why they are different:

Amphibians have smooth, moist skin that is sometimes sticky. Reptiles have dry skin with scales.

Both amphibians and reptiles can have legs and feet, but only lizards have claws.

Both hatch from eggs. The babies never know their parents.

A big difference is that amphibians mostly live in water. They lay their eggs in water.

Reptiles mostly live on land. They have to lay their eggs on land.

Where do geckos come from?

Wild geckos were first discovered in Asia, throughout Pakistan and in northern and western India.

Wild geckos do not make good pets.

This is a wild tokay gecko at a nature reserve in Thailand.

Today, leopard geckos are captive bred to be pets. Captive bred means they and their parents and grandparents were born and raised as pets.

They were never wild.

Wild Leos

Where would you go to find wild leopard geckos? The answer is the rocky and dry grasslands and deserts of Afghanistan, Pakistan, Iran or north-west India.

Though usually hot and dry, these places can get cold in winter. The temperature can dip to lower than 50 degrees F. (10 degrees C.) When it gets cold, wild geckos go to sleep in underground burrows. This sleep is called brumation.

During brumation, they stay alive because of the fat stored in their tails. When it warms up again outside, they wake up and come back to the surface.

How are wild geckos different from pet geckos?

Wild leopard geckos aren't as brightly-coloured as pet geckos.

Wild leos hibernate in the winter. Hibernate means they hide and sleep all the time in cold weather.

For lizards, this kind of hibernating is called brumation. (Here's how to say it: BREW–may-shun).

If your gecko seems to want to go into brumation, it might be that the room with the tank is too cold.

What makes leopard geckos different from other geckos?

Leopard geckos have brown spots on their backs and tails that look like a leopard's coat.

Unlike most other lizards, leos have eyelids. They can wink at you!

Leopard geckos have smooth, cool skin. There are bumps on their backs and their bellies are dry and smooth.

This is Tristan's leo, Gizmo, when he was 3 months old.

I Want A Leopard Gecko

Chapter One

Why can a Leopard Gecko be a Good Pet?

There are many types of geckos. Only some make good pets.

Leos are the best gecko to choose as a pet because they are more gentle, quiet and well-behaved than any other type of gecko.

They look interesting. There are lots of different colours and patterns.

Leos are sweet, friendly and easy to care for and keep healthy.

Also, they don't get very big. They don't need a lot of space for their home.

Leopard geckos don't need a lot of attention, because they are happy to be alone. You won't need to brush their coat or take them for walks. They will never chew on the furniture or break things.

Leos can live in a small space and are easy to feed.

Even though geckos are a small creature, they are fun to have. They will climb up in your hand to say hello. They're a friendly creature.

They could bite when they are very upset. If they do, you will hardly feel it.

This is a juvenile gecko. Juvenile [how to say it: Ju–ven-eye–ill] means not still a baby, but not an adult yet. Photo by Fouroaks via Stockfresh.

Leos will squeal when they are upset, but otherwise they are completely quiet.

Who would NOT enjoy having a gecko and why?

If you want a pet you can run around and play with outside, the pet for you is a dog. Geckos are an indoor pet.

If your family travels a lot, will there be someone back home to care for your gecko? Leos don't enjoy travelling.

It is not a good idea to have any type of reptile pet if there is a baby or child who is younger than age 5 in your family. It wouldn't be safe for the baby or young child, or for your gecko.

To own any pet, you need to be responsible.

Your pet is depending on you for food and everything else he or she needs.

Do you think you will give your gecko good care, even when you don't really feel like it?

Leopard geckos are crepuscular [here's how to say it: cray-pus-cue-lar].

This means they are most active just after sunrise. This would be about when you're waking up in the morning.

Their other active time is just before sunset, or late afternoon or evening for humans.

If you want a pet that is active during the daytime, a leopard gecko might not be the right pet for you.

Leopard geckos can live a really long time.

If you are age 10 now, your pet leo could still be alive when you are 20, or even when you are 25.

Are you sure you will always want this pet and will be happy to look after him or her for a long time?

10 Reasons Why Leos Make Great Pets

What are the advantages of having a pet leopard gecko?

1. Little leos don't need a lot of attention, like some other kinds of pets. They're content to spend time alone in their tank, just as long as they get some playtime with you each day.

2. They don't need to be groomed.

3. You never need to take them for walks.

4. They live in a smaller space than most other pets. Even a small bedroom has enough room for a leo's tank!

5. They're easy to feed.

6. They won't ever chew on your slippers or destroy your house.

7. They're a quiet pet.

8. They aren't smelly.

9. They're easy to keep healthy. You will hardly ever have to take them to the vet.

10. They live longer than most other types of pets. They can be your friend for a long time to come!

Chapter Two

Questions and Answers About Pet Leopard Geckos

How long do they live?

Leopard geckos that are pets usually live about eight to ten years. But some leos live as long as 20 years or more.

Males usually live longer than females.

How big do they get?

A baby leo is about 4 inches (10 cm) long. Adults are about 8 inches (20.3 cm) long. Males are usually a bit bigger than females.

Do leos change colour? What colours do they come in?

No, leos don't change colour. They don't get the spotted pattern on their backs and tails until they are adults.

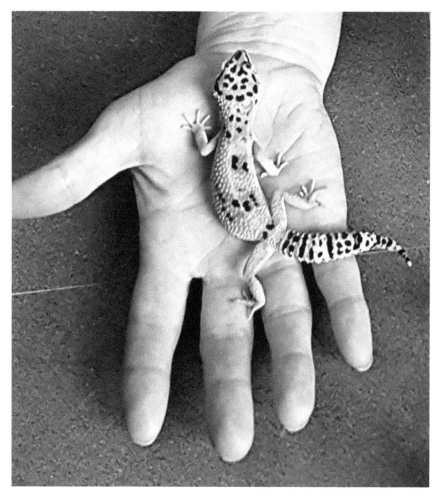

This is Gizmo when he was still a baby gecko. Photo by Doug Pulsifer.

Leos usually have a background colour of gray, yellow or orangey-yellow. They don't get their brown spots until they are adults.

Do leos like to be handled?

Most do after they get to know you, especially during their active times of day.

If a leopard gecko squeals or makes a hissing sound, it means you are not being gentle enough. Or it wants to be left alone right now.

You also have to protect leos from falling to the floor.

Playing with a young leopard Gecko.

Are geckos active?

Leopard geckos aren't very active during the day or at night. If they live in your bedroom, they won't wake you up at night!

The time when your gecko wants to see you, be active and eat is early in the morning or in the evening, during twilight. Twilight is the time when the sun is setting.

Are leopard geckos smelly?

No, they are a very clean animal. They always poop in just one corner of their tank. This makes it easy to scoop the poop and keep them un-stinky.

Can leos wag their tails?

Baby geckos can get so excited about being fed that they will wag the tip of their tails. Adults don't do this.

Are they poisonous?

No, but it is very important to always wash your hands with warm water and soap before AND after you touch a gecko. Just using hand sanitizer is not enough.

There is a very small chance that you could catch an illness from a gecko – or it could catch an illness from you.

This is baby Gizmo shedding. Photo by Debbie Pulsifer.

Do they shed their skin?

Yes, baby leos shed their skin almost every week. Adult leos shed their skin about once a month. Then they eat the skin. No one knows exactly why they do this. But it is very interesting to watch!

You will know your leo is getting ready to shed when his or her skin starts to look gray-ish. After shedding, a leo's coat is brightly-coloured again.

Is a leopard gecko a leapin' lizard?

Yes!

Geckos are curious creatures. They can move really quickly, especially baby geckos.

Sometimes they will try to leap out of your hands if you aren't careful.

If they do get loose in your home, it could be very hard to catch them again!

Can geckos see in the dark?

No creature can see when it is totally dark. But many animals can see better than people can when there isn't very much light.

In low-light conditions, people see everything as shades of gray. This means everything looks like it is lighter gray, or darker gray. We can't see in color when it's almost dark, but many animals can, including geckos.

Leopard geckos see blues and grays, and possibly also greens in low light. They probably can't see red.

Tristan with Nico. Nico is an adult female gecko.

How much time does it take to care for a pet gecko?

Leos take less time to care for than just about any other pet. Feeding them takes just a few minutes every day (for baby leos). Adults should only be fed two or three times a week.

You need to clean the poop in their tank often – once a day is good. This just takes a minute or two.

Their tank needs to be cleaned once a week. It could take 15 minutes or so.

You also need to take care of your crickets and mealworms. This takes just a few minutes every day.

How much help will I need from my parents (or someone older)?

You will need some help setting up the tank and getting used to caring for your leo.

Someone older will need to drive you to the pet store to buy more crickets and mealworms.

When to Go to The Vet

Take your leo to the vet or a reptile expert right away if:

- They are twitching or bleeding.
- They have lost weight in their tail.
- They won't eat and have no energy.

A pet leo in a nicely setup tank.

These problems are not as serious, but you might still need help if your leo has diarrhea, is constipated, or a toe or the tip of their tail turns brown or black.

My Leo's A Picky Eater

If your leo doesn't want to eat food from your hand, it might be they don't like how your hand smells. Always wash with unscented soap before you handle your pet.

A leo that won't eat can usually be tempted with live crickets to hunt in their tank, or mealworms. Sometimes, leos don't eat if they don't have enough

This adult leo is warming himself up on a nice, comfortable rock.

fresh water to drink. If they still won't eat, you may need to see the vet.

Chapter Three

How to Get Your Gecko

There are many ways to get a gecko.

Pet stores are a place to find your pet gecko. Or you could look online for a quality gecko breeder.

Or go to a herp show, where you will see many geckos offered for sale.

A herp show is a big trade show for people who have reptile pets, or want one.

Herp shows like the one this poster is advertising happen about once a year, usually in big cities.

Herp is short for herpetology [say it like this: HER-pet-taw-low-gee] Herpetologists are the scientists who study amphibians and reptiles.

You may have to travel a long way to go to a herp show, but it is worth it. You will see hundreds of awesome reptiles there, including leos.

These shows are very popular!

Today, all leopard geckos are captive bred. They are not captured wild animals that are imported into our country (and could bring diseases with them).

This means geckos you can buy are born to be pets.

Good breeders (the people who sell baby geckos and other types of reptiles) only sell healthy animals.

The Manitoba Reptile Breeder's Expo
September 24th & 25th, 2016
10am - 5pm
VIP Access 9am (Saturday Only)
Weekend passes available

Canad Inns Polo Park - Ambassador Rooms 1 & 2

1405 St Matthews Ave, Winnipeg

Tickets $10.00
Kids 12 and under FREE!

Tickets at the door - Info available online - Free parking

Presented by: **Winnipeg Reptiles & Prairie Exotics**

With top breeders from Winnipeg and across Manitoba!

www.TheMRBE.com

This is a poster for a herp show. The little guy at the lower right is a leo.

If you get tired of your pet, you cannot just let him or her go free in your back yard. This would be cruel, because they will not survive.

How much do pet geckos cost?

Depending on where you live and where you buy your gecko, it could cost from about $20 to $80 for a leopard gecko.

You should know that there are some very exotic geckos that sell for as much as $3,000! They are expensive because of their rare colours and patterns.

Who will pay for your leopard gecko?

One question parents always ask is, "But how much does it cost to have this pet? Who will pay for it?"

It's a good question because no pet is free to get or to have. Leos need two things that cost money. These are heat and food.

Heat comes from the heating pad or heat strips under the tank, or a light over the tank. These run on electricity, but it is a very small amount. So your family's electricity bill will go up, but not by very much.

Leopard geckos eat crickets and insect worms. These could cost $15 or $20 per month.

Before you get your gecko, you need to know who will pay for him or her.

A baby leopard gecko. Photo by Debbie Pulsifer.

How to get your Leo for Less Money.

If you want a leo but need your new pet to cost less money, here are some ideas:

1. Pet stores sometimes put tanks on sale. Or you could save money by buying a used tank. Look for ads in community newspapers and on free online ad sites to find a good used tank.

2. Most pet rescue shelters won't accept reptiles. But there are a few pet shelters that only take reptiles.
Look to see if there is one near where you live. They may have a little leo looking for a good new home.

3. Sometimes pet owners find they can no longer keep their pets. Look in local newspapers and online at free ads to see if there is someone who wants a new home for their leo.
Often they will sell their pet with the tank and everything that goes with it. Prices we've seen lately have been about $35 to $80 to adopt a leopard gecko from another pet owner, with the tank.

4. There are lots of ways to make hides that leos will love. Get creative!

5. You'll save money on crickets when you buy them online. They can cost even less when you raise your own instead of buying them.

Should you get a baby gecko?

Baby geckos are so cute! But babies always need more time and care than adults.

For one thing, baby leos need to be fed more often than adults.

With good care, a baby gecko will become an adult before he or she is one year old.

Should you buy two geckos so they have a friend in their tank?

Geckos are happy to live alone.

If you do decide to have two leos in the same tank, it should be two females. They should be about the same size.

You can't put a male and female together unless you want the female to have babies.

And you can't put two males together because they will fight and could hurt each other.

Which leo should I get?

Choose one that is in a clean enclosure and looks well cared for.

Your leo should have bright eyes and be active with lots of energy.

His or her tail should be as wide as the body.

A healthy leo's eyes should be bright and clear.

Try to be there when the gecko you want is being fed. A healthy gecko is a good eater.

You also want a friendly gecko, not one that squeals with fear when people get close. You don't want a scaredy-cat gecko!

Don't buy a skinny gecko or one that doesn't move very much because you feel sorry for it. A skinny gecko is a sick gecko that might not live very long.

<u>Chapter Four</u>

Getting Ready for Your New Pet

This little gecko looks like most of the leos you'll see at a pet store. Photo by Debbie Pulsifer.

It's best to have everything you need to welcome your gecko to his or her new home before you get your gecko.

You need a tank that is set up just the way geckos like. You also need the food they like to eat.

What kind of food do geckos eat?

Lizards eat live insects and nothing else. They will not eat fruit or vegetables.

Leopard geckos like crickets and insect worms (mealworms).

You can get these at the pet store or online.

Geckos also need to take their vitamins! Buy reptile vitamins, calcium and D3 powder at the pet store (or online).

The D3 might be in with the vitamins, or it could be in with the calcium.

Vitamins, D3 and calcium for leopard geckos are not pills. They are a powder.

You put this powder all over an insect by gently shaking the insect and the powder together in a small bag.

Then feed the powdery insect to your gecko right away.

Your feeder insects need to eat too.

Feed your crickets or mealworms with apple or carrot slices and oats.

If your gecko doesn't eat the insect or worm right away, take it out of the tank.

If you leave feeder crickets or worms in the tank and your gecko falls asleep, the insects could bite your gecko and injure him or her!

A leo resting on a warm rock.

What kind of tank will my leo need?

You need a tank for your gecko's new home. A 10 gallon (38 litre) tank is big enough to start with for one gecko. It is better for your leo if you get a bigger tank.

Geckos can't climb on a smooth surface like glass, so they won't escape from the tank.

There must be a screen lid on the gecko tank if you have other pets. A cat or dog might think your gecko looks good to eat!

There are several things you need inside a leo's tank

Leos need some heat in their tank! This is because leos must have belly heat to digest their food.

They also need a way to cool off if they get too hot!

There are two easy ways to keep your leo warm enough:

1. You could have an under-pad heater that goes underneath part of the tank.
2. Or, for extra heat you could use a light hanging over just one part of the tank.

Using either an under-pad heater OR a light over one part of the tank will give your leo the heat she or he needs.

If you use a light, it needs to be on a timer to turn it off at night and on in the daytime.

Leos are very stressed by having a bright light on all the time. Just like you would be when you want to sleep.

Leos love to have lots of places to climb up onto.

A climbing branch or pile of flat rocks is a good choice.

You can buy them at pet stores or online. Don't just use something you find outside, because it could have bugs or make your leo sick.

This is Gizmo's dry hide.

Leos like to hide

Leos must have dark places to go to be alone and rest or sleep.

These places are called hides because they are where a gecko goes to hide.

You will need three hides in your new gecko's home.

1. One hide needs to be dry and in the warmest part of the tank.

2. Put another dry hide in the coolest part of the tank.
3. The third hide can be in the middle. It is just like the other two, except that it needs to be kept wet inside.

One way to keep your wet hide cool and moist is to put some paper towel inside the wet hide. Put water on the paper towel so that it is always damp.

Rosie steps into her wet hide. The black cord in this photo is part of the tank thermometer. (A thermometer shows the temperature).

You can buy fancy hides at the pet store.

Or you could make simple hides that your gecko will be just as happy with.

There are lots of ways to make a hide. You could use a broken plant pot, bowl or coconut shell. Just be sure there are no sharp edges that could hurt your gecko.

You could create a hide out of a pile of flat stones. Or just use a paper towel roll for the dry warm hide or dry cool hide.

A hide always needs to be big enough for your gecko to get in and out easily.

A upside-down plastic food container with a hole cut in the side makes a good wet hide. Check that the hole you cut on the side is big enough with smooth edges.

When you set up the tank, be sure that there are no places where your gecko could get stuck, like between a rock and the tank wall.

Another thing you will need is a water dish that is easy for your leo to get into.

Sometimes, geckos want a bath so they can cool off. The water needs to be just deep enough to cover your leo's belly.

Get a food dish that is easy for your gecko to grab crickets or worms out of. You could buy a reptile food dish, or use a shallow dish that your family already has.

Or you could feed your gecko one insect at a time and watch him or her eat it. This way, you won't need a food dish.

Any leo would love to call this fancy tank his or her home!

Creating a great-looking tank is part of the fun of having a leo!

To make your tank more interesting, you could put in some plants in small pots. A gecko doesn't have to have plants in his or her tank, but they look good.

Leos really like to bask on a branch or a flat rock. Basking is when a lizard just hangs out in a warm place and takes a nap.

Leopard geckos can get bored with their tank and being in a small space.

Every three weeks or so, you should change around your tank's set-up. Moving the flat rocks, branches, hides and plants will keep life interesting for your gecko.

Here are four things you <u>don't</u> need in your gecko's tank:

1. **You don't need sand in the bottom of the tank**. Geckos sometimes accidentally swallow the sand with their food. This can make them really sick. Paper towel, flat rocks, pea gravel, astro-turf (this is fake grass) or nothing at all on the floor of the tank is a safer choice for your gecko.

2. **You don't need a heated rock** from the pet store. This is a bad idea to have because it can get too hot and hurt your pet.

3. **You don't need dried reptile food flakes**. Just about any leo will turn up his or her snout and refuse to eat it.

4. **You don't need gecko toys**. Leos like lots of places to sit, climb, rest and hide. They don't care about toys.

What makes the best floor for your leo's tank?

1. Reptile tile (you can buy this at most pet stores or online).

Rearrange your leo's tank each week after you clean it. This keeps it interesting for your pet.

2. Flat stone tiles
3. Astroturf or reptile carpet. Be sure to get the kind that your pet can't get their claws caught in.
4. Paper towels or newspaper.

Never use these: any kind of sand, including calcium sand. Don't use wood shavings, because it is poison to geckos. Don't use gravel because it can damage their skin. Don't use anything that is dusty, because they will have breathing problems.

Where to put your leo's tank

Put your leo's tank in a place where you can enjoy seeing your pet all the time.

In your bedroom is fine if your bedroom is always the right temperature for a gecko.

The tank needs to NOT be next to a heater or in direct sunlight. It's just too hot!

Leos also need no lights on at night.

Leos like a quiet life. Lots of loud noises will make your gecko sick.

If you like to make a lot of noise or need to practice playing the drums in your bedroom, your leo will want to live somewhere else.

Bringing your new leo home

A small ice chest works to bring your leo home from the store.

When you get home, gently release your leo into the tank.

Don't feed your gecko until the next day.

Leave him or her alone to explore and get used to their new home.

You should give them at least one week to get used to their tank before you pick them up.

I Want A Leopard Gecko

Chapter Five

How to Tame Your Gecko

At first, just put your hand down in the tank. Let your new pet get used to you slowly.

A curious leo who is ready to make friends will come over to your hand and might even climb onto it.

You will need to be patient with a baby or nervous gecko. It could take a month or longer for your gecko to feel comfortable being touched and ready to come out to visit with you.

Like all pets, your leo needs time to get to know and trust you.

Be very, very gentle with your leo!

Never grab your leo or squeeze him or her.

Handle a leo like you would a brand new baby kitten or puppy.

Never pick him or her up by their tail.

Be really careful not to drop a pet leo!

Remember that loud noises or you moving suddenly frightens them.

You need to be calm and quiet when you are holding a gecko.

Don't be surprised if they poop on your hand.

Just put them back in their tank and wash your hands right away with soap and warm water.

One safe way to handle your gecko that both of you will enjoy is to let them crawl hand-over-hand when you sit on the floor, or on the couch.

What could go wrong with your new pet?

Usually, very little can go wrong with a pet leo. They are easy to keep healthy and happy.

A leo that gets too fat needs to keep eating crickets but eat fewer superworms. Use superworms only for a treat, once a week.

Feed baby geckos every day. Adults need to eat three times a week.

A very skinny leo that has no energy is sick. You might need to take her or him to the vet.

Be careful not to let insect worms or crickets bite your leo. If your leo doesn't eat an insect or insect worm right away, don't leave the insect in the tank.

If you want to have two geckos, they must be females. Each gecko needs her own places to hide. Geckos do not want to share! If you have two geckos, you need six hides. You also have to be sure that one gecko isn't taking all the food.

For two geckos to be comfortable and happy together, you need a bigger tank.

Stop! Don't kiss that lizard!

It is safe for you to have a lizard pet and handle it. It is NOT safe to kiss your lizard.

Don't do any of these things, because it's not safe:

1. Don't handle your pet and then touch your face.
2. Don't clean your pet's tank or <u>anything</u> from the tank in the kitchen sink or in the bathtub.
3. Don't forget to wear rubber gloves when cleaning the tank or anything in it.

The reason NOT to do all these things is that you can catch a cold or the flu. You could get sick from touching your gecko if you're not careful.

The way to stop this from ever happening is to ALWAYS wash your hands carefully. Do this with warm water and soap before you handle your leo and also right after.

Keep your pet away from people food and where your family cooks your food.

This is important to help keep you and your leopard gecko healthy. Having a sick pet – or you or someone in your family being sick – is just no fun for anyone.

A leo on a small glass globe.

This is Tristan with his best lizard friend Gizmo. In this photo, Gizmo is about 6 months old.

Chapter Six

What to Name Your Gecko

Are you wondering what to call your new pet? If so, here are some ideas.

You could give your gecko a 'people' name, like Molly or Sam.

You could find a name you like in your favourite movie or book. You might pick a name like Minion or Snape or Rango.

Maybe the name you like is from TV – names like Smurf, Muppet, or Geico.

Or it could just be a word you like – or even a word you make up!

Here are some more names for your pet leo:

Dragon	Bolt	Cookie
Princess	Widget	Sprout
Cuddles	Geek	Cupcake
Blondie	Burp	Squeaky
Bungee	Widget	Flash
Jujube	Gummy-Bear	Baby
Twinkle	Sprocket	Mr. Big

Leopard geckos can be a wonderful pet!

This book doesn't tell you everything you (and your parents) need to know about pet geckos.

If you are interested in reptiles and excited about getting a leopard gecko, you will want to read lots more about them. This book has given you everything you need to know to get started.

We hope you have a happy time getting to know your new pet leopard gecko!

With good care, you and your leo could be best friends for many years to come!

Best wishes,

Tristan and Jacquelyn

Got a question or comment about leopard geckos or any kind of pet? Want to tell us about your pet leo? Write to us here:

Jacquelyn@CrimsonHillBooks.com

Tristan@CrimsonHillBooks.com

More Fun Books For Kids Who Love Pets!

Read more great pet books from Crimson Hill Books!

Best Pets for Kids series:

I Want A Leopard Gecko

I Want A Bearded Dragon

I Want A Puppy Or A Dog

I Want A Kitten Or A Cat

Fun Animal Facts for Kids series:

Fun Dog Facts For Kids 9-12

Fun Cat Facts For Kids 9-12

Fun Leopard Gecko and Bearded Dragon Facts For Kids 9-12

Fun Reptile Facts For Kids 9-12

Fun Pets for Kids series:

Small Fun Pets: Beginning Pets For Kids 9-12

Top 10 Fun Pets for Kids 9-12

Investigate more books for curious kids right here:

www.BestPetsForKids.com

CPSIA information can be obtained
at www.ICGtesting.com
Printed in the USA
LVHW07*2255260618
582042LV00015B/54/P